Anonymous

Literary clubs of Indiana

Anonymous

Literary clubs of Indiana

ISBN/EAN: 9783337306083

Printed in Europe, USA, Canada, Australia, Japan

Cover: Foto ©Thomas Meinert / pixelio.de

More available books at **www.hansebooks.com**

Literary Clubs of Indiana

By Martha Nicholson McKay

Indianapolis
The Bowen-Merrill Company
1894

TO THE DAUGHTER

WHOSE PRESENCE INSPIRED AND
WHOSE HELP LIGHTENED ALL THE WORK
THIS LITTLE BOOK IS INSCRIBED
BY HER

GRATEFUL MOTHER

Indianapolis, Indiana.
November 22, 1893.

The Literary Clubs of Indiana.

The Literary Clubs of Indiana.

CHAPTER I.

FIRST INFLUENCES.

Causes of Organization—Earliest Efforts—Helps and Hindrances.

Of all the states, not one was more difficult to make habitable than that ideal home of the Indian, well named Indiana.

The dense forests, later the source of wealth, must by Herculean efforts be cleared away that the sun might bring new wealth to the new fields. The settlement of Indiana's towns and future cities was most perilous. At the risk of life, between the dangers of the tomahawk on one side and the deadly malarial fevers on the other, the first cabins were roofed, and the first corn fields returned their harvests.

Later, the opening of the West, and Northwest, caused emigrants to look beyond Indiana. The prairies were bleak and wind-swept, but they yielded crops at once without the infinite labor of clearing a farm.

And so it came that the picturesque trains of white covered wagons—this pathetic history still unwritten—which before the days of railroads were constantly winding from East to West, over the great National Road, stopped no longer in Indiana; but moved beyond her bor-

ders to found the homes which should be the strength
and glory of the great nation.

Thus Indiana was often deprived of that most valuable
citizen, the New England or middle states settler; while
the central and southern part of the state became an extension of Kentucky and Tennessee, the emigrants bringing with them the habits and ideas peculiar to those states.

Yet, as if the law of compensation must be demon-
strated in Indiana, we find that, while as a state her
growth was retarded by early illiberal tendencies, race
prejudices, and timidity in regard to America's chief sin,
she held within her borders the seeds of future moral and
intellectual life in a far greater degree than her neighbors.   The ground-swell of Europe, its significance noted
by Kant and later interpreted, somewhat differently, by
Robert Owen and his followers, was agitating the new, as
well as the old world.   While the United States was com-
paratively little known to European scientists and phi-
losophers, the southern part of Indiana was famous by
reason of the socialistic experiment at New Harmony.

It was indeed an enterprise to impress the world, if to
the ears of the multitude the purpose could have been
spoken; Robert Owen, wearing still the laurels of his
wonderful success at New Lanark, emphasizing his zeal
by the gift of his fortune, coming to the new wilderness
of a new world to apply the Golden Rule to daily life.

The man who counted his friends among the best of the
English nobility, and to whom kings and presidents alike
had given attentive hearing, coming with touching sim-
plicity to offer all—time, money, ability, unceasing personal effort—to reform the ills from which society suffered.

The material life of New Harmony's Socialistic Experiment had a short and restless existence of three years.
The ideas of its founders, with the hopes they sustained,

are here to-day, not alone in the village on the Wabash, but in the state, in the nation, in the world. Shall we see what New Harmony did for Indiana? Although himself an incessant traveler, Robert Owen drew and held men of distinction and great learning, and many of them spent their lives in the interest of science and of philanthropy in this modest Indiana town.

The "Father of American Socialism," as Robert Owen has been called, ended the earthly life where it began, in the well-beloved native land; but to America, and for years to Indiana, he bequeathed his gifted family of four sons and one daughter. His son Robert Dale Owen, representing his county successively several times in the state assembly, and a member of the committee to draft its constitution, was instrumental in giving whatever superiority Indiana had over the prevailing prejudices of that time. It was he who made it possible for married women to hold property in their own right and in their own names.* He secured from the government that fund of over half a million, the interest of which goes toward sustaining the public schools. Indiana is wont to boast of her "largest school fund," forgetting that, perhaps, of all the states, her need in that direction is largest; forgetting, also, to name the hand which was first stretched forth to apply the state's money to this best of uses. Later, when representing his state in congress, it was Robert Dale Owen who introduced the bill and secured its passage, establishing the Smithsonian Institute. And much later, when there was scarcely a rift of light in the clouds that hung above our civil war, it was his letter to President Lincoln, the letter so full of logic, of tenderness, of courage, that caused the trembling scales to droop toward the side of justice and

* For information indebtedness is acknowledged to History of New Harmony, Dr. J. Schneck and Richard Owen.

national salvation—and the proclamation of emancipation was written.

To another life-long resident of New Harmony the present method of teaching geography in the primary grades is due, but Richard Owen, a younger brother of Robert Dale, has not yet been fully credited with this honor; indeed, so many and so famous were the scientists here, that abroad New Harmony was known as the "Scientific Mecca."

Prince Maximilian, when traveling in the United States in the years 1832–34, spent a week at New Harmony, the grateful guest of those whose intellectual attainments swept away all distinctions of rank.

Sir Charles Lyell also praises this town in the published volumes, giving an account of his geological explorations in the United States in 1841.   He writes:

"Many families of superior intelligence, English, Swiss and German, have settled in this place.   *   *   *   We were glad to hear many recent publications, and some of the most expensively illustrated books, discussed and criticised here."

Thus, it appears that before the plea was made by the serene philosopher in Concord, Massachusetts, "plain living and high thinking" were in existence in New Harmony.

Here also lived Joseph Neef, teacher of Pestalozzian principles and author of the first book on pedagogy published in the United States.   From another citizen, Wm. McClure, came the provision by which $100,000 was set aside to found libraries for working men throughout the state.   That the townships of Indiana did not appreciate the gift, that it was at that time a case of throwing away pearls, is not creditable to the state.

In 1839, Dr. David Dale Owen was appointed United

States geologist, with headquarters at New Harmony. It was he, who, by the aid of those whom he appointed, and who worked under his supervision, made the explorations in the northwest, ordered by Congress. "This Herculean task was accomplished in two months, and the report laid before Congress at the opening of its next session," writes the historian. New Harmony continued to be the headquarters of the United States geological survey until 1856, when, upon the completion of the Smithsonian Institute, they were transferred to Washington, D. C. The immense and exceptionally rare and valuable collections accumulated by Dr. Owen were divided. A part was taken to Washington, D. C.; another part to the Indiana State University at Bloomington, and a third portion to the American Museum of National History in Central Park, N. Y. Said a noted geologist: "In passing through the Smithsonian at Washington, and the museum at Central Park, I was surprised to find so large a proportion of the specimens, in all departments, labeled as coming from the New Harmony collection."

Ideas require time in which to germinate. That the germs of truth scattered so lavishly in Southern Indiana more than half a century ago, and falling oftentimes upon barren or hostile soil, had an influence, and a very powerful one, thoughtful students no longer doubt. Even now that early protest for the higher needs of life, the love of Art, is bearing fruit.

While the Art Association of Indiana's chief city, with its more than one hundred thousand citizens, has no abiding place for the few pictures it owns, a citizen of New Harmony who came with Robert Owen a penniless lad, is building for the town at his own expense a commodious art gallery in which his own gift of pictures, to the value of over seventeen thousand dollars, will be a constant joy

and help to the privileged citizens.   These pictures, many
of them classical subjects, were selected in Europe with the
aid of America's famous artist, W. N. Story.   Some of
them were found in Florence, and the whole forms a collection of which any great city might be proud.

CAUSES OF ORGANIZATION.

It is a curious fact that civilization progresses by waves.
First a great religious or moral awakening; then a period
of intellectual activity, when all questions must be an-
swered by reason, and looked over by the light of a scientific lamp.   Now it is the spiritual life alone which is of
consequence, and again it is this wonderful mechanism,
the human body, the temple of the spirit, which we ex-
alt.   The senses must have opportunity for perfect development.   Recently England's spiritually minded art
critic declared that intellectual activity was dependent
upon good cooking.   The causes for literary organization are the same as those which prompt organization for
material or mechanical work.   It comes in answer to a
request for help.   The man alone can not accomplish
what he comprehends may be done.

But organization, coming as it apparently does in the
natural order of things, is yet always dependent upon
some waiting, watching soul, who first realizes the need,
and takes the first step.

When Indiana was a wilderness neighbors met to help
each other in a material way.   They joined their physical
strength to raise the heavy timbers for house or barn.   To-
day, when iron vitalized by steam has so lightened the
labor of man, we can scarcely realize the difference between our own day and half a century ago.

" How did people hear from each other then?" asked a
little girl recently.   "Wrote letters, paid twenty-five cents

postage, and waited a month for them to be received," replied her father. But now, by the magic of electricity, our country instantly asks and answers its thousands of questions, important and insignificant. The development of the material interests of the country forces people to become specialists. There is neither length of day, nor length of life, to do what many a scientist would like to compass. In this life it is scarcely possible to learn to do one thing well. And so the specialists must organize and combine, that each may bring his share, and in helping all, himself be helped.

All this is true of the invisible work of mind. So much to learn! so short the time this work can command! We must divide into groups, or study alone, and then combine for the distribution of our literary wealth. Another cause for organization for literary work was found in the mental and moral stimulus which followed upon the close of the war. When the first demoralizing influences inseparable from war had passed away, it was found that in the hearts of sorely chastened people there was a renewed love for justice and liberty, and that wider charity which follows these two virtues. It is fitting here to call the attention of those who suppose the civil war a fiery baptism lasting only four years, to a few now seldom remembered facts. Before the visible conflict, lasting from 1861 to 1865, this nation wrestled in moral warfare for thirty years. The spirit emanating from New Harmony in the person of Robert Dale Owen could work beneficent results for his own race, but even his loyal hand could not keep from the statute books of Indiana the blot of her Black-laws. Within her borders not fugitive slaves alone, but free colored men coming from other states were hunted as were the wild beasts in her forests.

While the material wilderness of Indiana was penetrated in quest of material wealth, into the moral wilderness of custom and public opinion came at a very early day the anti-slavery pioneer, planting in peril and in personal affliction the precious seeds which to-day are blooming and bearing fruit. This work was, in this state, largely in the hands of the Quakers, only a few shining examples of moral courage being found in the Campbellite or Christian and Methodist churches.

These are the people of whom Lowell wrote so long ago—

> "All honor and praise to the women and men
> Who spoke out for the dumb and the down-trodden then!
> It needs not to name them, already for each
> I see history preparing the statue and niche."

In Indiana, as in other places, the first steps toward organization were taken for other than literary purposes. Before the war, political and religious barriers were kept in good repair. Politically, men and women were arrayed for, or against America's chief sin. Religiously, the close communion Baptist scorned the wider hospitality of the large-hearted Methodist; and the Presbyterian, clinging to conservative traditions liked not to hear the voice of a woman in outward prayer. It may be the foundations for a later union for intellectual work were laid when the loyal women of Indiana met to roll bandages for the horrible possibilities of expected battles. A common anxiety, too often a common sorrow, made them friends. Later, the union religious meetings which followed the close of the war, their very existence confessing that all morally earnest people had their faces set toward Zion, made it possible for a future co-operation for intellectual work upon that high plane above all sects and creeds. So rapidly has public opinion changed, we forget what a great thing it was, when the former Puritan influence, which had per-

secuted and banished other sects, was swept away by the
invitation to join all sects and creeds under Evangelical
leadership. The movement was too thoroughly Trinitarian
to be just, but it was a great step forward.

Again, the wider outlook for women, the growth that
comes from trial, the experience bought with a price, all
these ploughed deep the fields which to-day are so rich in
the promise of a future harvest.

EARLIEST EFFORTS.

Perhaps the first regular meetings for literary culture
among women were the early reading circles where the
company listened to one reader, until a later accumulation
of confidence made them able to take part in discussion,
or in turn become reader and director.

The first clubs for men were few, and were inspired by
the influence radiating from some college or college man.
Mixed clubs for literary work were not known in Indiana
until the theory of co-education had found adherents.
Most helpful were those few college societies where young
men and women mingled in debate or literary criticism.
Necessarily these influences reached beyond the college
doors into the wider school of life. Unless a comparison
could be made, it is not known how materially the early
club life of Indiana differs from that of other states.
There were a few notable instances in her early history.
She has the honor, so far, of having the oldest woman's
club in the United States. One of the literary societies
of Hanover College is fifty-three years old; and one of
Indiana's mixed clubs is twenty years old. Three literary
clubs for women were organized in 1874, but associations
for literary work did not come in great numbers or enthusiasm until many years later.

The first strong impulse was recognized in 1876. Perhaps the Centennial awakened state as well as national pride. About this time in Indiana, as elsewhere, questions of political equality were discussed. As if in preparation for new duties and a wider outlook, the zeal for mental growth among women far exceeded that among men. They were on the outposts, looking over the field, noting what would be needed when they came to possess the land. And yet almost universally the organization waited for and depended upon some one earnest spirit, for people are led to ideas through personal feeling, confidence in, and affection for, leaders. Around some clear mind and courageous soul these new ventures clustered in almost every instance. While Indiana as a state had solved few of the great questions of the time, within her borders, a step was taken which advances her to leadership in the club movement, at least in regard to clubs of women. Neither Massachusetts nor New York can claim the honor of establishing the first woman's club. The friendly rivalry between Sorosis and the New England Woman's Club may continue, but to neither can be given honors due the first born. The first successful effort to establish a woman's club in Indiana, and, so far as is now known, in the United States, was made in New Harmony in 1858. It was organized by Constance Fauntleroy, a granddaughter of Robert Owen. But recently returned from a residence abroad, with the influences of school and university lingering in her mind, she gave to the club the classic name of Minerva. Thus every succeeding woman's club can point with satisfaction to the wisdom of its ancestry, and remember with renewed reverence this first attempt to bring to the women of the new state the culture and mental growth so valuable.

The life of this first club was short, yet quite long enough to point the way to other literary organizations. Miss

Fountleroy was a native of Indiana, born in Indianapolis in 1836, a fact which will add to the pardonable pride of the club women of the state.

After the organization of this club, doing such valiant work, verily announcing in the wilderness the great movement that should follow, there is an interval of many years. During that memorable decade, this state, in common with the others, had known the bitterness of civil war and the blessedness of peace; a peace not bought at the expense of national honor and Divine justice, yet paid for even to the uttermost farthing in National discipline, in personal sacrifice and sorrow.

At this time, 1872, the College Corner Club of Indianapolis was organized, its membership including both women and men. It is believed to be the oldest mixed club in Indiana.

Two years later, 1874, the Woman's Reading Club of Greencastle, the Ladies' Literary Society of Evansville, and the Woman's Literary Club of South Bend were organized; Greencastle's club being the oldest of the three.

As far as the limits of so brief a history will admit, some of these clubs will receive a more extended notice.

Helps and Hindrances.

The early efforts of lyceum bureaus and the influence emanating from the lecture platform were efficient aids to later organizations for literary work. These advantages Indiana did not enjoy as did some of the other states; yet, to her chief towns and principal cities, came more or less frequently the shining lights of the pulpit and platform. Emerson stood before very small audiences; those who were thus privileged, then, little dreaming of the great honor they enjoyed, yet every one of his hearers, blessed and strengthened, if unconsciously, by the calm and beautiful presence of the man.

Recovered from the brutal assault of slavery's representative, Charles Sumner stood before an Indiana audience, his matchless explanation of what the nation should be and the possibilities it had, making those who listened dedicate themselves anew to the work then before American citizens.

Wendell Phillips' golden sentences were heard from time to time in the state. Mrs. Livermore, in her marvelous lecturing tours, made almost uninterruptedly for twenty-five years, came annually to Indiana. Equally at home with historical, biographical or reformatory subjects, her presence as well as her words gave a wonderful impulse to the organization of women for self-improvement and for work in all reforms.

The agitation consequent upon the woman's suffrage movement, and the wide-spread work for temperance, often gave an impulse which crystallized into an organization for literary work. Sometimes the members of these associations were extremely conservative; nothing of a reformatory or heretical nature must be whispered in the club; and it came about in many instances that, in the faithful study of literature alone, members found they had only taken another road to Rome. In a few years, from some of these first, very conservative clubs, came quite radical reformers.

The rapid development of all material interests, the better facilities for travel and rapid communication, the improved postal service—all these were helps to organized literary work.

A noted politician and ex-governor of Indiana asserts that the financial storm and panic of 1873–4 greatly aided the intellectual growth of the state. In his view, the prosperity since the war and the rapid acquisition of money were moulding the people into wealth-worshipers, and when their wealth was suddenly swept away, they turned to find the treasures which are neither to be lost nor depreciated in value.

It is true a wave of literary organization followed the financial cloud. While societies and clubs for literary work have been steadily increasing since 1878, the greater number in later years points to one great help in forming new clubs, and that is, it has become the fashion. The early abolitionists, instead of diminishing, as might be expected in the natural order of events, are, as their early work becomes popular, marvelously increasing. And now, those clubs which were first in the field are jealously watching other clubs, lest the now highly-prized honor of age and the precedence due to it be displaced by some inexorable date. Do these well-satisfied present members ever recall the chilly atmosphere that almost congealed the hopes and plans of those who launched the ship in which they now sail with such complacency and satisfaction?

Another help in organizations, noticeably so in the formation of woman's clubs, is the personal attraction to and love for leaders. Several clubs are thus named for women who have been honored in this way.

Limiting the membership of clubs has sometimes been the cause of organizing a new club. People most desire the unattainable, and women finding no room in the organization to which they would like to belong, generally form another club, into which enters the stimulus of harmless rivalry.

The Indiana Union of Literary Clubs, organized three years ago, has now fifty-two clubs in this Union, and applications for admission coming constantly to the secretary. This has no doubt been a great help to literary organizations. As an instance: At the convention held in La Fayette in May, there were several representatives from clubs in Fort Wayne, and before six months had passed, there were organized in Fort Wayne alone five new clubs. The confederation of clubs has, also, had its influence in stimulating literary work in the several states, Indiana among the others.

These are some of the helps to organization. What are the hindrances? To those who sought to organize woman's clubs fifteen years ago, the air was full of warnings: "Duty lies at home with children by the sacred fireside." "Would you exchange the protection given to modest womanhood for any degree of intellectual strength?" This was the frightful handwriting on the wall, that ever and anon appeared for solution. And to those who first sought to organize a purely literary club for men in Indiana, what mountains of business engagements, and cheap wit, and dreary humor, they encountered! But when, in the fullness of time, this work was called for, to the pioneer in this unexplored region strength was given. In organizations of women, often the chief hindrances to helpful work rest in the women themselves and their much to be deplored methods. Responsibility, the sense of power, affect very differently different people. While it subdues some women, emphasizing their natural conservatism, to others it gives an intense desire for power and leadership. Many women, now forbidden political fields, display an alarming aptitude for wire-pulling and caucus scheming. Some literary barques have been very nearly wrecked by the unworthy ambition of self-appointed commanders. Again, very like children with a new and wonderful toy, have been the actions of some club women. The club work was seen alone through their personality; their friends, their set, were the most desirable for membership. A majority of the clubs for women, men, and for both, have narrow and imperfect rules in regard to the admission of members. While it is true that clubs, to do the best work, should be harmonious, and composed of those who have "unity in diversity," it is also true that women often handle black balls with a reckless disregard for justice and the fitness of the candidate. Very often, ruled by personal and unworthy motives, feelings of bitterness and dislike which a generation may not see fading, have been engendered by this lack of conscience, coupled with a little "brief authority." But let not organizations of women be counted the only ones in which this relic of the dark days of Venice lingers. Clubs composed of men, and mixed clubs, show the same weakness. Said a member of a large mixed club in a large city of Indiana: "The best people in the place, those possessing every qualification for membership, have been black-balled in great numbers by the efforts of two or three vindictive or ambitious members." In many clubs with a large membership, three negatives exclude. Are these the evils that must needs come? As men and women learn to work together in the ever-opening and ever-widening fields of the intellectual life, it is to be hoped that in the light of a wider culture these dark practices will disappear. In the hands of a representative membership committee, the question of new members and the harmony and usefulness of a club need not come into conflict.

Some of the women's clubs suffer from the ponderous machinery of the constitution under which they work. Much valuable time is often consumed in asking and answering questions in regard to the lawfulness or unlawfulness of some new machinery in the form of by-laws or amendments to the already long document. It is very

true that women need to know much more about parliamentary law than the average woman does know. The
knowledge thus gained in club life has been very valuable; but in many instances the awful zeal they have shown
in watching the constitution and by-laws has left little
time and strength for the literary exercises.

"I joined a class to study Emerson," said a young woman
living in a large town in the state, "but three-fourths of
our time was taken up in the discussion as to the pronun-
ciation of words, and this was so distressing to me I could
not remain." Thus was the spirit lost in the endeavor to
perfect the form.

There is before me the constitution of a woman's club,
having seven articles, which include sixteen different sections, eight by-laws, and seven amendments. The first
by-law reads: "The meetings of the club shall be held
at half-past two (sun time), on Saturday of each week
throughout the year. * * *" Again, in the by-laws:
"No member shall absent herself from a meeting of
the club during its sessions and previous to adjournment, unless excused by the president." It would appear
that the members of this club were bound with all the
rules and regulations which the old-time method put
around their school days. And in addition, no vacations,
for, unless special action was taken, every Saturday of
the year was club day. In restful comparison to these
hard-working club members, many organizations report
working helpfully, with few rules, and some clubs have
no officers, the lady at whose house the meeting is held is
the president for the day.

This is notably true of the Reading Club, of Fort
Wayne. This club meets at the homes of the members,
and the hostess is president.

In response to circulars sent out for information replies

such as these came from fifteen large and flourishing towns in the state : "No club in this town." "I am sorry to report that there is nothing of the kind in this county." "No literary organization here; have plenty of talent, but do not seem so inclined." It is believed that when attention is called to this lack in certain localities interest will be awakened.

CHAPTER II.

KINDS OF ORGANIZATIONS.

Professional—Social and Literary—Lecture Associations—Chautauqua Movement—Reading Circles—Farmers' Organizations for Literary Work.

This is the day of organization. Wherever a profession is represented by several people, they are quite sure to organize. They elect officers, adopt a set of rules and wheel into line with the countless other associations great and small.

Among the laboring classes in cities and larger towns, both women and men are members of organizations designed to promote, at least, their material interests. To these organized centers a degree of literary culture has already come in the form of addresses delivered by those who represent in their lines that social culture and education which makes it helpful not only to hear them speak but to see their faces as well. Those whose lives are devoted to literary pursuits are generally members of some one of the recently formed clubs. The Press Club is a feature in the literary associations of Indiana. It yields both profit and pleasure to the journalists, authors, editors who have united in obedience to the present impulse for organization.

It might be expected that social clubs would preclude literary clubs, but it is not always so in the villages and towns of Indiana. Where there are social clubs they are often identified with literary work. Many of the earlier organizations were committed to a social feature. In some instances this was discontinued, and again clubs have set apart certain sessions where refreshments are served and the social side of club life considered. In the cities and larger towns of Indiana the musical people have, for several years, combined and organizations known as musicales have greatly aided in perfecting musicians and in a better appreciation of good music by the citizens. A majority of these musicales are organizations of women, but they form a center round which musicians, both men and women, gather, often combining to give entertainments which greatly aid those who give and those who receive this pleasure. The fact that they have a literary feature in the study of the lives of great composers, and the growth of the different schools of music, gives them a place in this monograph. These organizations have been the means of bringing rare musical talent into localities where, but for their preparatory work, it would not have been possible.

If Indianapolis and Evansville led in this work, the younger cities are not far behind.

In Anderson there are two strong musical societies, both composed of women: the Matinee Musicale, with fourteen members, and the Lyric, with thirty members. Most encouraging of all, there is, in the same place, a society composed of twenty little girls, calling their organization the St. Cecelia. They are taking their first steps in musical culture, with the advantages that come from united effort and its attendant enthusiasm.

LECTURE ASSOCIATIONS.

There was a time when in Indiana, as in other states, the Lyceum was the people's college. The lecture associations of this state were, in certain localities, many and

well organized. Naturally, they flourished most in
and near the college towns. Many of the early literary
clubs made it a part of their work to secure at least a few
valuable lectures during the year. If the lecture associations for the last few years have not been crowned with
the old-time success; we may conclude that the many literary clubs have supplied the want, and perhaps have
taken the place of the earlier work of the lecturer. But
there are still many lecture courses organized in connec-
tion with literary work. Of these the University Extension maintains its high ideal along educational lines.

Eight years ago, in Plymouth Church, Indianapolis, a
plan was originated, and soon executed, by which the
best lectures were brought within the hearing of those
with limited means. The object was to bring the best and
newest thought to the people at the lowest price. Course
tickets for five, and sometimes six lectures were sold for
one dollar. The committee were satisfied if in this great
educational work expenses were defrayed. The lectures
were the best that could be secured; the subjects varied,
including science, as well as the discussion of the various
vital questions of the hour. From time to time the programme was lightened by the best musical talent or character delineations by the noted readers before the public.
For years the lecture course of Plymouth Church was considered one of the most helpful experiences of the year.
So far as is now known, it was the first effort in this
direction, and has been widely imitated in this and other
states. This plan of popularizing the best thought of the
time influenced many of the Y. M. C. A. organizations, en-
riching their work and enlarging their influence in a non-
sectarian way.

Plymouth Institute, one of the organizations connected
with Plymouth Church, Indianapolis, deserves mention

here as being the first of similar efforts now existing, and
to be multiplied in future. Its object is to give literary
culture with practical instruction to those whose opportunities have been limited, and to that larger class prevented
from finishing the course provided by the public schools.
An extract from the secretary's report for last year will
best explain its worthy aims.

PLYMOUTH INSTITUTE.

"This evening Plymouth Institute enters upon its ninth
year of usefulness in this community. During the past
eight years it has had an enrolled membership of up-
wards of twelve hundred, and an income of about three
thousand dollars. It has had classes for the study of Reading, Writing, Arithmetic, Book-keeping, Elocution, Short-
hand, Drawing, German, French, Ancient, Modern and
Current History, General and English Literature, special
classes for the study of the writings of Homer, Dante,
Shakespere, Goethe, Carlyle, Hawthorne, Lowell, Emerson, Browning, Spencer and George Eliot.

"Its travel club has wandered over Holland, crossed the
Alps, and visited the charmed cities of the sunny South.

"Large classes have studied Civil Government, Social
Science, Physical Culture and Singing.

"An important course of lectures, organized specially for
the young people of this city, have been given each year
on some subject connected with American History, fitted
to make them speak plainly the word country.

"Its teachers for each class have been thoroughly qualified in every particular for the special branch undertaken
by them, while its lecturers have each made a special
study of the subject treated by them.

"Its reading-room has been supplied with the choicest
selection of American and English current literature.

"When the Institute was formed no similar opportunity
was offered the citizens of this city. Now there are up-
wards of a dozen. It has, besides, stimulated the formation of small clubs throughout the city for the study of
special subjects, mainly literary. It was the forerunner,
and made possible the success of the University Extension
movement in this city. Similar institutions have been
formed along its lines in cities stretching from the Atlantic
to the Pacific, and from the Gulf to the Lakes. Its work
has drawn forth expressions of the highest praise from
Oxford professors, and distinguished men and women in
our own and other lands.

"All its members, I believe, cherish happiest recol-
lections of the Institute, and rejoice in the friendships
formed."

CHAUTAUQUA WORK.

The plans recognized by the well-known initials C. L.
S. C. were first perfected in 1878. Five years before, in
1873, the "Society for Culture at Home," organized in
Boston, Mass., had influenced many minds in widely sep-
arated localities. Individuals or associations of three or
more began to read systematically and under wise guidance. These, at first faint lights, shone far into the intellectual wilderness of the West and South. Some of those
first organized efforts exist to-day in the Ticknor Clubs
registered in the "List of Organizations."

The Chautauqua Work, compared to the independently
organized work of clubs, must bear the relation of school
life to the life of the individual after the doors of school-
room and college have closed. The classes in Chautauqua
are marching under orders, never breaking ranks to ex-
plore the regions round about. All this is well for those
who can not, or will not, grow mentally without this aid.
And has not Chautauqua proved that there are thousands

who must be so registered? The existence of the Chautauqua plan is the argument most in its favor. "Forty thousand persons pursuing the outlined course; thirty thousand having completed it." Several members of the classes are over eighty years of age; in this work renewing their youth, finding in this way, proscribed though it be, the intellectual hygienics resulting from system and regularity. These facts are interesting and suggestive.

The arguments against Chautauqua are not many. Perhaps the chief one is that the work must be necessarily superficial. In answer to this comes the frank statement of its committees: "C. L. S. C. does not claim to be a substitute for either high school or college, and does not afford what is implied in a liberal education." An argument against the methods of C. L. S. C. was recently given by one certainly interested in the intellectual advancement of Americans. A protest was entered "against popularizing history or science." A regret was expressed that the books written for Chautauqua were written down to the level of children instead of being kept up to the full stature of manhood.

From a necessarily short study of the methods of C. L. S. C., it appears that the machinery, however indispensable, has undue importance. At a recent meeting of one of the oldest circles, the ground covered by the programme was alarming in extent. In this one evening they went over Greece at one of the most interesting periods of her history; then a comprehensive (?) view of America's relations with foreign powers, and, although, the hour waxed late, it was proposed to take up a wholly different subject for the finale. This work was done by reading, without comment, from slips of paper upon which were recorded names and events, which, to the student of world history, meant volumes. It was like having a brief sight of stereopticon views passed without the connecting links of explanation. They may remain in the memory, but without the use which an understanding of their relative meaning would give. The remedy for this might be the introduction of more original work, and the practice of free and full discussion of such work by the members. Thus would freedom of thought and mental strength "grow by what it fed on."

Chautauqua is sincerely unsectarian. To the student of religious evolution, it is interesting to note the proportionate number of denominations in her enrolled classes. In one class, given as a typical one, where the enrollment was twenty-five thousand, the denominations stood thus: Methodists, six thousand seven hundred; Presbyterians, three thousand five hundred; Congregationalists, two thousand six hundred; Baptists, two thousand two hundred and seventy-five; Episcopalians, one thousand three hundred and seventy-five; Roman Catholics, two hundred; Friends, two hundred; Unitarians, one hundred and fifty, and the informant added "many other denominations, from Universalists to the Salvation Army." There were in this class six thousand students who gave no denomination, presumably members of the great church outside of those who work under a name. This number of the religiously unnamed, constituted almost a fourth of the whole class. This fact of itself gives Chautauqua good and sufficient reason for existence—this union of all former stout defenders of creed and those of no creed, by its existence acknowledging the supremacy of the intellectual life.

The plans of Chautauqua for helpful mental and spiritual growth, combined with bodily recreation in the summer schools or assemblies, are worthy of great praise—that reminder of another and no less important need of man, rest from mental weariness by change of mental food; the opportunities for interesting young people in science, in music, in literature, while they are in that happy receptive mood which a vacation and change of surroundings furnishes; hearing lectures by those men and women whose very presence is helpful, whose useful lives are the diplomas they most prize—all this is work of which the council may be justly proud.

Without a knowledge of the extent of C. L. S. C. work in other states, it is believed that Indiana has had her full share. In sixty of her ninety-two counties flourishing circles have been established and circles are still organizing. Of the eighty-three established circles known to date, sixty-eight are active, and the fifteen reported inactive should be credited to the full for the work they may have done. If Chautauqua work has paved the way for the organization of independent literary clubs, may these clubs, in grateful recognition of pioneer work, show these circles the value of individual and original work. Listening to the honest criticism from friendly lips, may the Council of C. L. S. C. direct the readers to the most helpful sources, giving them books, undiluted, with no longer the fear lest the food be too highly concentrated. Especially is it to be desired that in the important department of religious literature, a council confessedly undenominational, no longer exclude from recommended lists such rare and helpful books as Lydia Maria Child's "Progress of Religious Ideas" and James Freeman Clarke's "Ten Great Religions."

A few years ago the importance of beginning with the children and young people, the cultivation of a healthy desire for literature and the more practical sciences was realized by a few earnest members of the State Teachers' Association. It is said the directing thought came from

Marshall county.   Be that as it may, the various plans
crystallized in the formation of the Young People's Reading Circle.   As the best and most comprehensive statement of this work, the following is given from the pen of
Miss Baylor, of Wabash:

    *   *   *   "Recognizing how greatly the complete men-
tal growth depends upon proper courses of reading, and
realizing the need of direction in such lines, not only for
children but for teachers, the Teachers' Association of
the State of Indiana, at their annual meeting in 1883,
decided to organize a Teachers' Reading Circle, and a
board of directors, consisting of ten members, was appointed to direct this work.

"The remarkable success of this circle led the same association in 1887 to establish a Children's Reading Circle
for the guidance of the young people in the state.

"We recognize errors in social life and attempt to remedy
them.   Vexed questions of labor are now presenting themselves, and various theories in lines of socialism and
anarchy are devised for their interpretation.   What these
will do, it may take centuries to determine, but their ulti-
mate value must be estimated by their contribution to the
growth of society.   So with the reading circle.   Its es-
sentially good nature must be measured by results; yet we
need not wait centuries for those since they are already
shown, even beyond our sanguine hopes.   For the Teacher's Reading Circle in this state responds to the number
of ten thousand; and already one hundred thousand children have allied themselves with the Young People's
Circle.   Our teachers, by reason of books read, have taken
up systematic lines of study and have broadened in a way
that a school training could not possibly effect, while the
increasing sale of such books as Fiske's Civil Government

and The Autocrat of the Breakfast Table, shows a marked improvement in literary taste.

"The culture of the young people through their reading is most evident to the teacher, and beautiful letters filled with spontaneous expressions from the children of the state to the secretary of the board of directors have shown the pleasure these books give, and the great and important office this organization is destined to fill in the mental development of our young people. Like our World's Fair, these circles have evolved from feeble beginnings.

"Parallel with it, they are bringing their members together socially, extending good into families, social circles, and states, until seeing their past prosperity, and on that basis alone predicting their future, we can say without hesitation, that the representation of these reading circles as factors in the evolution of that society which we are ever tending to elevate, is worthy and essential."

In February, 1891, steps were taken toward the organization of Farmers' Reading Circles. Several have been established, and the expectations of the most sanguine have been realized. A list of seventeen books was recommended the first year. This list embraced many books which would completely change the often monotonous trend of the farmer's mind. Awakening an interest in science, and art, through Ruskin's Ethics of the Dust; in poetry, through Whittier's immortal idyl of Snow Bound; in tenderness toward animals, and a new view of the relationship of man to all nature, through the pretty story Black Beauty; the chemistry of the farm, made by Warrington as interesting as fiction, and yet solid with truth. All this gives great promise for the future.

The president of a Farmers' Reading Circle writes: "Wherever local circles have been organized, they have proved to be both a means of pleasant recreation and an aid to the social and intellectual improvement of farmers' families. * * * The meetings in the farmers' homes afford an opportunity for the young people to become accustomed to the usages of society; also to become somewhat familiar with parliamentary law—an accomplishment that is far too little appreciated in our rural districts."

CHAPTER III.

LITERARY CLUBS.

Number of Associations—Memberships—Women's Clubs— Men's Clubs—Mixed Clubs.

Many circumstances have combined to make the list of clubs numerically somewhat imperfect. The indifference of those from whom the necessary information was sought; the indifference in some instances of clubs in the matter of being recorded, and the constant formation of new clubs —these conditions would render any list but the most recent incomplete.

At this date, the whole number of literary organizations in the state, found by actual correspondence with officers or members, is one hundred and seventy-nine. Of these one hundred and eight are women's clubs, twenty men's clubs, and forty-six mixed clubs. The great disproportion in the number of organizations for men and women is significant. It may mean not only that women are seeking to improve, but also that when the day of larger social and political freedom dawns, they will be prepared for the new duties the wider field may disclose. That culture which comes from organized effort, the faithful study of subjects, aside from all religious or political bias, is coming to the women of Indiana. This is the story the club lists tell: Of the twenty clubs for men alone, ten are college societies, making a still greater difference in the number of clubs purely literary.

Interesting and valuable as all literary work must be in

these separate clubs, the mixed club is the ideal one, and may well be called the club of the future. Here questions can be discussed in the truest light. that given from two standpoints, for many questions must appear very differently to men and women. Only the duality of eyesight can give perfect vision. The mixed club makes possible the full and free discussion of questions which neither men nor women can see perfectly alone. Here can the fabled shield be turned until the side of silver is recognized as of equal value with the side of gold.

Hammerton says: "I think that the greatest misfortune in the intellectual life of women is that they do not hear the truth from men." And from this statement we must conclude that this gifted English critic was never a member of a mixed club. From Indiana's forty-six mixed clubs much is hoped for, and already much has been realized.

WOMEN'S CLUBS.

The examination of the programmes as well as constitutions and by-laws of women's clubs, proves that they are, at present, disciplinarians to a fault, and they have brought to organized literary work great fidelity and conscientious effort. They emphasize the duty of performing the exercises arranged for. Many clubs make unexplained failure in the performance of duty for three or more meetings, sufficient cause for losing membership. In one club the member has the alternative of paying a fine of fifty cents. Other clubs have wisely decided that the preparation for and performance of duty can not have a relative money value, and refuse to consider fines. One club meets weekly through the entire year, providing for adjournment only by a majority vote. Their club day is Saturday—in the old days set apart for women's

work, but not club work.   Many clubs meet on Monday,
another day rescued from old-time dismal associations.

In a large number of clubs, the exercises begin by re-
sponses from each member.   These are from some author,
or are original sentiments in regard to some popular
question.   It seems to be a sort of preliminary course for
the intellectual feast which follows.   In many clubs each
meeting has a musical number on the programme.   Some
of the new organizations vary the exercises with recita-
tions; but the older, and we must believe, the most helpful, clubs arrange for serious consecutive work, satisfied
with a smaller field, well cultivated.   In fifty programmes
examined, there were but three found which included
regular religious exercises.   One opened each meeting
with reading a psalm; another a Bible reading; the third
had "Scripture reading, followed by the Lord's Prayer
repeated in concert."   That this very large proportion of
clubs organized for literary work should arrange a purely
literary programme means no irreverence.   On the con-
trary, we should infer that the true effect of religious
culture is that continual recognition of right thinking
and right living, and needs not constant reminder by an
external form.   **1544259**

In many programmes of the current year a Columbian
tendency was discernible, many devoting the first meetings to the study of subjects relating to the Exposition.

Upon some clubs the argumentative spirit seemed to
have descended, and for one or two meetings a debate
upon some popular topic was arranged.   This may be
well enough for the sake of experience, but the free discussion by all members of one leading paper is certainly
more beneficial.   It is interesting to note the growth of
the older clubs, manifested in the work they choose;
how they leave the first enchanting fields of biography

and history and turn toward scientific questions or social
problems.

One club has devoted much time to botany; another
studies political economy during the whole of this year.
This is one of several organizations taking no vacation.
While the majority of those who compose literary clubs
are resting at home or summering abroad, this club is
discussing "Fundamental Truths of Political Economy,"
"Importance of Railroads," "Advantages in Division of
Labor," etc. During 1892–93 they discuss "Taxes—
Direct and Indirect," "Strikes and Trades-Unions,"
"Supply and Demand," "Co-operative Associations."
If they faint not by the way, the women of this club will
be much better qualified to vote intelligently than the
majority of the men who deny them equal political privileges.

An afternoon club has upon its programme these sub-
jects: "The Indian's Side," "The Race War," "The
Russian Press," "The Electric Age," "A Glimpse at
Evolution and Darwinism."

The Tourists' clubs in many places are interesting.
Studying a locality together is like traveling in good
company. A Conversation club in Anderson is endeavor-
ing to revive an art which was a few years ago about to
be consigned to the lost arts. The bright and interesting
subjects which appear for discussion on their programme
bid fair to do great credit to this club, which has the first
meeting of each month devoted to conversation. Another
club in this same growing young city provides six "guests'
meetings," finding pleasures shared are pleasures in-
creased. This club, the Edgerle, is exceptional in the
matter of members' names. In the list, both the given
name and name before marriage is retained by the married members. The vexed question has been solved by

this club doing what in its simple and sweet dignity con-
vinces by the eye as well as the intellect, for the members' names look as beautifully as they read sensibly. In
the programmes of thirty-eight women's clubs, sixteen
gave women's names in both lists of members and on the
programme. Of the remaining twenty-two, three gave
the husband's given name in both the members' lists and
on the programme; the nineteen remaining gave the
married member her own name on the programme and
her husband's given in list of members.

Another interesting fact is the large number of clubs
recently organized. In the women's clubs organized in
the years between 1888 and 1892 it was found that more
than one-third were formed in the last two years, fourteen
being organized in 1891 and twenty in 1892. The same
proportion will, it is thought, be found in mixed clubs,
but not in clubs for men alone.

If the influence of clubs for literary work is beneficent
in cities where there is so much to stimulate the mind,
with what double blessing will this work come to the agricultural districts. "As iron sharpeneth iron, so does
the face of man his fellow" is not too old a proverb to
have its vital relation to the life of to-day. There are recorded two very interesting clubs for women, which are
working outside of town or village, the meetings held at
the different farms of the members.

One of the members wrote: "We desired to improve
and saw no other way, so eight women met and organized
this club. It is often very difficult to attend, having
sometimes to walk over three miles to the meetings."
When we remember that the leisure season for country
people is the winter and that Indiana roads at the best are
not like the old Roman highways, we can estimate the
zeal it requires to keep the club well attended.

The other country club has put quite definitely the two
sides of life in its name, for it is called the Mary-Martha
club, and the motto is the "Actual and the Ideal." On
the outside of their programme they have printed the
words spoken so long ago to the sisters at Bethany, and
from a perusal of their outlined work, it is evident they
are trying to choose the better part.

MEN'S CLUBS.

Of these, as shown in the list of organizations, Indiana
has ten clubs and nine societies belonging to her colleges.
Of the latter, Hanover has the oldest, her two societies
dating back to 1830–32. Of the clubs, Crawfordsville,
Indianapolis and Peru have each two, the remaining four
belonging to Bloomington, Greencastle, Richmond and
Terre Haute. One of the Crawfordsville clubs is interesting by reason of the name as well as from the character of its members and the line of work. Its historian
tells us that it was, upon its organization, in 1883, called
the Crawfordsville Literary Club, and under that name
had a pleasant and useful existence of four years. In
1887 it was reorganized under the name of Ouiatenon
Club. We read: "The name was chosen as a memento
of the early history of Indiana, and in memory of the
Ouiatenon tribe of Indians, who once inhabited that part
of the state." This evidence of sentiment in a club composed entirely of men reconciles one to the task of trying
cheerfully to pronounce the name of their organization.

The Gentlemen's Club, of Greencastle, also enjoys the
advantages which a college town possesses, and among its
members are the professors interested in scientific as well
as social questions.

MIXED CLUBS.

Of these clubs, correspondence has been held with forty-six, and it is believed that all have not reported. The weakness, the imperfections, if such there be, in the separate organizations for women and men vanish in the mixed club. Their reports are always full of promise for their future work and satisfaction with the work accomplished. One of the most interesting of these clubs discloses in its name loyalty and state pride, and the Hoosiers, of Rockville, organized in 1887, may well appear in its line of work, its interest and its influence, a standing argument in favor of mixed clubs. A woman is president of the club. Her description of the organization is also good evidence on the side of these clubs. She writes: "Ours is a mixed club. We find it very helpful to have our husbands with us. We also think we do them good."

The Tourists' Club, of Richmond, is another very large and interesting club. They began this year to travel through England, later taking a look at England's colonies. At each meeting two papers were read and discussed. It is pleasant to see by the programme how evenly the honors and the duties are divided between the men and women. The thought that the few societies which can be mentioned are but types of the many others gives great cause for satisfaction.

CHAPTER IV.

TYPICAL CLUBS.

Women's Clubs.

The oldest existing club in Indiana, and at this time believed to be the oldest women's club in the United States, is the Alcuin, of Madison. Its history is best given in the following extract from the letter of Mrs. M. Sears Brooks, of that city, a member of this soon-to-be-famous organization. She writes: "The Minerva was organized by Miss Fauntleroy, in New Harmony, in 1858. After her marriage to Rev. James Runcie, and her removal to Madison in 1861, she called a few friends together and organized the Bronte Club, adopting the same constitution she had drawn for the club at New Harmony. The Bronte was composed entirely of women. Mrs. Runcie was its president. * * It was purely a literary club, and furnished original matter in the form of stories, poems, sketches, etc., for the entertainment of its members, and some of the better articles were published. A few years later the club reorganized, and admitted men to membership, and for several years, and perhaps its most successful ones, flourished under the name of the Phœnix. Through death and removal, another change seemed desirable, and the club reverted to its original status, that of a woman's club, and then adopted the name of Alcuin, in honor of him who first thought women capable of receiving instruction, and hence became the tutor of Charlemagne's daughter. The course of work embraced after this change included historical research and literary culture, and was pursued with great thoroughness. All officers and fines were abolished, the meetings were held at the residences of members in rotation, and the hostess acted as president of the evening.

"This plan has been pursued up to the present time and is objectionable for but one reason, the absence of any record of proceedings. Our membership at first in 1861 numbered about a dozen women; in its mixed member-bership as many as seventy-five were on its roll; and when composed of women alone, has numbered as many as thirty. It has been called a close corporation because no one was admitted without full consent of each individual member. Removals by death and otherwise have brought our membership to its original number, twelve. We take great pride in our club as being the oldest existing club in the state, perhaps in the United States. The New Harmony Club, organized in 1858, was not sustained for any length of time; whereas the club in Madison has held its regular meetings uninterruptedly, save for summer vacations, ever since its first organization, thirty-two years ago, and its membership now includes those who were active in its promotion in the year 1861."

Indiana has not only the oldest woman's club, but the one which fulfills the highest conditions of a woman's literary club. In number, the apostolic twelve; in harmony, complete, its members those who work together with no dissent in regard to admission; the little brief authority an office gives shown in its true light by the abolition of all offices, proving that in the highest union for literary work there exists no need for encumbering official machinery; the abolishment of fines, a recognition of the higher law and newer gospel. There is but one mistake; a club so rich in the experiences which only time can give should keep a record of its work for the help and encouragement of the hundreds beginning the same journey.

WOMEN'S CLUB OF GREENCASTLE.

From the interesting history given by the secretary, we learn that it was at the home of Miss Ames, on the night of February 14, 1874, that five thoroughly in earnest women took council together. Did they reflect that it was a time sacred to St. Valentine? We do not know, but we find that early in the March following, to use the secretary's words, "the frail craft was then and there launched, and in May a constitution adopted." To quote again: "The subjects on the programmes for the first years were exceedingly miscellaneous, covering a wide field. We hesitated at nothing. No doubt our reckless-ness has often called to mind the proverb, 'Fools rush in where angels fear to tread.' But we were dauntless. We have learned a little as the years have rolled. In 1880 we began a regular course of study and have con-tinued it ever since." This is the interesting history of the oldest of the three clubs of 1874, the other two be-longing to South Bend and Evansville. Thus, almost twenty years ago, the state was not without three wit-nesses, prophesying of her future wealth in clubs.

INDIANAPOLIS WOMAN'S CLUB.

In the days of its youth, in that ignorance which was bliss, this club believed itself to be the pioneer. The days were far off which should by the unanswerable arguments of dates and records take away the honor it would be glad to possess. This organization, sixth in point of time, is yet believed to have been the first to abandon all explan-atory and propitiatory terms, such as "Literary," "Ladies" and "Society," and organize under the brief and simple name Woman's Club.

The first meeting was held in Mrs. McKay's parlor on the afternoon of February 18, 1875. That meeting, so small in numbers, only seven women prevailed upon to risk so much, represented many weeks of earnest effort upon the part of the three or four persons first anxious for the organization.

It would be almost impossible for club women to-day to realize the difficulties which lined the way when this work was begun. Some of the reasons for not wishing to be identified with a movement so new were recorded in the form of letters to the lady whose house had been chosen for the organization of the club. "I find my mission in taking care of my several little girls, and I do not wish for other work. Nor do I think I could either give or receive help by aiding your project," wrote one. Experiencing a change of mind, if not of heart, this very skeptical sister, years later, came into the club. "I should think you could see that your God-given duties point in another direction," wrote another sincere, well-meaning woman, whom it was believed would feel honored by an invitation to join. And so in the face of infinite explanation and information, giving repeated assurance that it was not the purpose to form a suffrage society, or a branch of the then newly organized temperance crusade; that its work would not be irreligious; that it was not likely to be followed by strange climatic changes or terrestrial convulsions, or immediate mental revolutions, seven women, in most sincere and serious mood, founded the Indianapolis Woman's Club.

The coming years were to reveal that it was not always clear sailing. How gently did the programme committee pilot through waters known to harbor dangerous rocks.

How the more conservative were appeased by papers on the newest discoveries in domestic science, or the always fruitful theme of how best to govern children. In the discussions which followed this last subject, those led who were rich in theories, without practical knowledge, while the mother who had sung her baby to sleep in order to attend the club was silent.

Looking back upon the organization of this club, it is now clear that the conditions surrounding the six early clubs of the state were very different. The liberal influences from New Harmony colored the Madison and the Evansville clubs. In South Bend the Eastern and Middle state atmosphere of the inhabitants made its impress. In Greencastle the influence of the college town was felt; but Indianapolis in those days was celebrated as a place where minstrel shows flourished—where Emerson's audiences might be counted at a glance. If the light from this first small lamp appeared rather dim, it was from atmospheric causes partly, and in part the fault of the lamp's construction. Like many another venture, it was the first desire to popularize it. Nothing could be more disastrous, as the years proved. Members sought for social position or large bank accounts did not stay. If in that early and vigilant search for members, the committee had but reflected, "Be ye not unequally yoked;" but they heard no voice like that. From the first there were the two elements—one devoted to the sincere and faithful study of large problems, the other turning toward subjects which concerned society in its outward forms rather than its inward needs.

> "And one impelled, and one withheld,
> And one obeyed and one rebelled."

Then came years when the club wrestled with little

points in the constitution, while great and waiting questions were passed by; days when Cushing's and Roberts' rules were exalted above the Golden Rule. But in all these tests, the result proved the foundations were upon solid rock. The winds subsided. The club stood. Only pleasant memories cluster about the early and unpopular days. Those who had first desired the organization stood bravely together for its interests. Those were the days when in honor preferring one another, the life of the club was their first thought.

Of the seven who first sat together in that meeting eighteen years ago, but one has passed beyond the earthly vision:

> "Lured by the sweet persuasion of a Hand,
> Which leads her somewhere, in the distance, still."

One, in the inevitable rush of Chicago life, often returns in thought and loving memory to those first meetings; and one from the peace and quiet which reign over a New England farm, turns from the sight of mountains and the distant sound of the sea, to sigh for the helpful companionship of the early club days. From the number seven, the club now places its membership limit at one hundred. Its influence has gone out to inspire new organizations throughout the state, many finding its constitution suited to their needs. In peace and prosperity this club now engages in the discussion of themes suited to its age and dignity. Free to look toward the problems this century offers, finding at last in its diversified composition a source of strength, it bids fair to climb upon the Augustinian ladder of the past into a useful and beautiful future.

Of the Tourists' clubs, the History class of Richmond deserves mention. Mrs. Dennis, who was instrumental in its organization, thus describes it: "Our class was organized three years ago, the charter members numbering thirty. Now we have nearly four hundred. Our membership is unlimited. We have bought one of the best stereopticons obtainable, and the ladies have learned to manipulate it with technical skill, using it each alternate week—one week history proper, the next illustration. We are now traveling in Egypt. We have but a small membership fee, but easily meet all our expenses. The members are loyal to the work and to each other. The high and beautiful ideas we are gathering into our lives are a constant inspiration to us all, and we feel as though we would be glad to work on another thousand years. It is seldom in a small city so large a body of intelligent mothers and daughters (and I may say granddaughters), for the ages run from sixteen to seventy, meet as often as once a week to discuss problems in history and art, especially if these problems are as old as Egypt."

Another very new and interesting club is one among many others in Fort Wayne. This club, called the Romanesque or Scott class, is now journeying in Scotland. Writes the leader: "If you should require a guide through 'Auld Reekie,' call upon any member of this class, fourteen in number (Jew, Catholic, Protestant), and I can vouch for a good guide."

The question as to whether social and intellectual joys shall mingle in the club has been solved by "Over the Tea Cups," an Indianapolis organization. After the completion of the literary exercises, tea and wafers, or cake, are served. This club also allows its members to "invite a friend" without the usual restriction of "being a resident from out of town." The sweet friendliness and dainty hospitality of this club lingers an ever refreshing memory in the minds of those priveleged to have been its guests.

MEN'S CLUBS.

Of these, the Century Club, of Indianapolis, judging from its programme, might be the modern typical club for men. Its range of subjects so wide, the topics being always determined by the writer's preference. In its practices, the spirit of its constitution is faithfully observed. Sections 2 and 3 of Article VIII read: "The essayist shall select his own subject and be free to express any opinion whatsoever thereon." "The club, as such, shall express no opinion on any subject." Its membership includes all sects. In a most friendly and helpful investigation, they discuss the questions of the hour. The descendant of the Huguenot here sits beside the Catholic priest, and the zealous Methodist and the Free Religionist find much common ground.

To refer again to the wide difference in the number of clubs for women and men—the former numbering one hundred and one, the latter ten—it would appear that by the law of compensation, a single club in the latter list should be ten times as strong and wise. The investigation of programmes and their subjects will not for a moment warrant such conclusion. Lists of members taken away, judged by the subjects for consideration, the programmes for women's and men's clubs could not be distinguished, but by the programme itself—the printing, the look, the arrangement—the difference is marked. The committee for clubs of men appear to leave their programme in the hands of the printer, much as the average man leaves his coat to the judgment of the tailor. The programmes for clubs of women are, many of them, daintily printed and gracefully adorned with sentiments that suggest new and wide fields of thought to all who turn their pages.

MIXED CLUBS.

For a fair type of these most to be desired clubs, the one believed to be the oldest in the state, has been chosen, and this is The College Corner Club of Indianapolis.

The name is a local one—College Corner being once an incorporated suburb of the city. Organized in 1872, this club has moved along for twenty years with very little constitutional machinery. The offices are few and the honors equally divided between men and women. Its membership has always included those, not only of widely differing views but those of different pursuits as well—judges, lawyers, physicians, men of business, women with the cares of family, and from time to time a good representation of America's nobility—teachers in the public schools. Its programmes, purely literary, have covered a wide field. In common with most literary clubs, the earliest efforts were in the direction of English literature, or history and biography. Leaving this work behind, this club gave several years to the study of Shakespeare, later, George Eliot's novels. Later still they studied the works of Goethe, and then lived again in ancient Greece, giving most careful and conscientious study to the works of the Greek poets. At present they are making the acquaintance of Plato. Among the members of this club, from time to time, were many who have since become famous as educators or scientists. The president of the well known California University took his first flight as a poet when a member of this club. The professor of languages in a Michigan college first delighted his hearers with his silver sentences, when they were all club members together. The president of one of Indiana's universities was for a long time the presiding officer of this club. Another college professor, when appointed secre-

tary of the club, took a new departure, his minutes rival-
ing in delicate yet irresistible humor the best of Mark
Twain's works. From time to time this club has been
privileged to entertain men and women distinguished in
the world of letters.

At one time the Bishop of Vincennes, but recently a
member of the Pope's household, gave to the club a lecture upon Art in Rome. In the discussion which followed those mingled who held views ranging all the
way from free religion to the Church of Rome. If, as
many believe, the mixed club is to be the ideal club of
the future, when, in that far distant time, historians
look back for first specimens, no doubt this first of Indiana's mixed clubs will receive its share of attention.

In the meantime its members, associated so long ago
for the best of all pursuits, are not insensible to the
privileges so long their own. Although the ranks have
been broken by the claims of duty and the experiences of
life, a majority of the first members are working still,
bound together now by years of association and pleasant
memories. And still, as the years go by, faster now than
in the earlier days, these fellow travelers in the journey
of the intellectual life find new pleasures and new strength
in exploring the ever-widening fields of thought.

CHAPTER V.

INFLUENCE IN CULTURAL DEVELOPMENT OF THE STATE.

The things that are seen are temporal; only the unseen is eternal. The memory of these words of St. Paul, coming to us from a time so distant, should ever deepen the conviction of the importance of the intellectual life, and the value of all organized effort in bringing that life nearer. In the number of Indiana's literary organizations known to date,* what power for mental growth is foreshadowed. Remembering that a promise of success and reward is given where even two or three gather in sincere and worthy endeavor, how this power is multiplied in the one hundred and seventy-nine clubs of the state.† Some of these clubs have a membership of one hundred and over; but few have less than fifteen. Taking the actual average, which is: Women's clubs, thirty-four; men's clubs, thirty-seven; mixed, thirty-six, we have five thousand three hundred and eighty-eight people united in one work, a work lifted out of all narrow claims and into the region where the universal good is the one thing sought. This estimate of club membership does not include any part of the many thousands who take Chautauqua work, nor does it include that immense gain being derived from the Teacher's and Young People's Reading Circles, or the few

---

* Several organizations are known to exist whose names and dates it has so far been impossible to ascertain.

† This includes the college societies.

organizations among the farmers. In these purely literary organizations it is well that a variety exists. Those who feel that women can best advance in societies exclusively for women will be pardoned for the pride they must feel in the knowledge that these clubs number now one hundred and one, with eight college societies. Others who have faith in mixed clubs will hope that the forty-six already existing may be many times multiplied. Just what action will be taken by those who believe in men's clubs, when they find the number but ten (ten college societies excluded) in the one hundred and fifty-seven clubs, can not now be foretold.

Among the many signs of promise, not one is more radiant with coming light than the desire for organized literary work in the agricultural districts. "The Farmer's Reading Circles will save us," said a thoughtful student of social problems. Only those who have lived the life know the complete isolation of a large farm and the need it discovers for mental stimulus and mental food. Social scientists are discussing the problem, "Why the sons of farmers refuse to stay upon the farm." Puritan Massachusetts mourns that the ownership of her precious soil has passed from the children of Americans and the deeds are recorded in the names of Erin's sons.

No more in all our land can be found a picture like that of Joseph Bonaparte mingling the grace and refinement of courtly manners with the duties of a farmer's life. We have no counterpart to that picture of General Washington greeting the rising sun, in the careful survey of his much loved farm.

And yet country life is only monotonous and uninteresting because those having eyes see not, and are unmindful of the privilege they possess in dwelling so near to nature's heart. What possibilities of mental and moral growth are enfolded in these prospective literary associations among the farmers! What hitherto denied companionship the list of recommended books discloses! No longer shall they remain strangers to art, science, poetry, or that new life the best of fiction reveals.

With what new vision the young man fastens the traces to the plow after reading "Black Beauty!" What new friends come with the morning light and linger in the evening shadows after studying "Life and her Children!" What enlarged views and renewed sense of responsibility comes to the student of "Fisk's Civil Government!" All this mental growth and finer spiritual insight is promised in time by this new work. While the literary work in agricultural districts may be prospective, this can no longer be said of the club influence in the state. It has already given a standard to other organized work, both religious and philanthropic. The meetings of the Minister's Union are taking on a literary hue. The missionary meetings have introduced other than accounts of mission work, in the form of carefully prepared papers, historical or biographical. The character of the Sunday night sermon, in a large proportion of the churches, has been changed. The doctrinal discourse has given place to studies of the vital questions of the hour, or to studies of helpful lives, and congregations are asking that literary merit, as well as intrinsic value, shall be considered.

The few but very valuable art associations of Indiana are associated with literary work in many instances. They have also had their influence in popularizing the illustrated Sunday night sermon, by means of which the best works of the best masters have been shown to those who could not otherwise enjoy them.

As yet Indiana has not needed to solve the great problem met in dealing with the ignorant and criminal classes in great cities. But there exists in her chief cities and larger towns quite enough material to justify the experiment which science and philanthropy desire to make.

"Idleness is only dangerous to the unintellectual," writes a thoughtful man, and the hope has been expressed that from the free reading rooms and evening classes may come that first impulse toward a higher life, which must aid in the reformation of the now dangerous classes.

In this love for healthy, hopeful literature these poorly fed minds shall begin their new growth. These belated souls begin to unfold. They will, perhaps, join together, and with the multiplied strength that comes from organization and co-operation press on, leaving the clouds behind, and together walk steadily towards the light.

In this united effort to reach the intellectual life, in this wider recognition of the dual nature of man, we read anew, by the electric light of the nineteenth century, the true and touching words of old: Man can not live by bread alone.

LIST OF ORGANIZATIONS.

WOMEN'S CLUBS.

Location.	Name.	Date.	Fee.	Mem.
Anderson	Clio Club...................	1890	$1 00	
	Edgerle Reading Club........	1885	Fines	16
Aurora..........	Mary Lyon Literary Society ...	1892	25	
Auburn..........	Ladies' Literary Club.........	1882	1 00	
Brazil....	Aftermath.	1892	N.	19
	Ladies' Literary Society.......	1878	....	24
	Woman's Reading Club........	....	....	26
Bloomington	The Coterie.................	1891	Ass't	40
Bloomfield.......	The Athene.................	1892	....	15
Cambridge City ..	Helen Hunt Club.............	1889	....	22
Camden..........	Woman's Literary Club......	1888	1 00	19
Carlisle	Tennyson Club.............	1882	N.	
Crawfordsville...	The Athenian..........		....	35
Connersville	A. D. O. U ...	1892	1 00	12
	The Connersville Cary Club....	1891	50	25
Clinton	Woman's Review Club.........	1892	N.	
Decatur..........	The Shakespeare Club........	1882	....	
	Ladies' Historical Reading Club	1889	N.	16
Evansville.......	Ladies' Literary Club..	1874	2 00	20

Location.	Name.	Date.	Fee.	Mem.
Fort Wayne....	Duodecimo. ...	1892		
	French Literature Club........	1892		
	Morning Musicale	....		
	Romanesque Scott Class.......	1892	N.	
	Saturday Circle...........	....	....	
	Seven Club...................	1888	N.	7
	Wednesday Club..............	....		12
	Woman's Reading Club.	....	....	32
	Shakespeare Club.............	1892	3 00	
	Unity Club........	1892	N.	
Frankfort	Tourist's Club................	1888	1 00	30
	Woman's Club..............	....		20
Franklin.	The Know-Nothings...	1891	85	
Greencastle	Woman's Club...............	1874	2 00	30
Greenfield........	Hesperian Columbian Club....	1889	50	
	Woman's Club................	1888	....	
Greensburg.......	The Cycle....................		....	
Indianapolis	Clio Club...................	1878	25	30
	The Fortnightly..............		3 00	75
	Katherine Merrill............	1885	5 00	59
	Magazine Club...............		...	
	Minerva Club.	1889	1 00	18
	Over the Tea Cups...........	1891	1 00	25
	Sketching Club.............		1 00	18
	Woman's Club...........	1875	4 00	100

Location.	Name.	Date.	Fee.	Mem.
Irvington.........	Woman's Reading Club.......	1892	N.	15
Knightstown.....	The Shakespeare Club..	1889	...	15
La Fayette	Afternoon Club...............	1880	...	18
	Monday Club...............			29
La Porte........	Woman's Literary Society.....	1878	....	24
Madison	Alcuin......	1861	N.	12
Marion..........	Woman's Conversation Club...	1890	5 00	53
	Arm-Chair Reading Club......	1892		14
	Philomath...................	1891	5 00	30
Martinsville. ...	The Shakespeare Club........		N.	
Milton	The Cary Club...............	1880	N.	
Muncie	Mary and Martha Club.... ...	1891		28
	Monday Afternoon Club.......	1892		15
	Woman's Club...............	1876	1 00	45
New Albany......	Amaranth ..	1884	50	
	Ephemnon ..	1891		25
Petersburg	Woman's Club................	1892	N.	
Peru	Susan E. Wallace Club.......	1892	50	50
Portland.	Shakespeare	1890	50	
Princeton	The Tourists.	1892		
Rensselaer	Ladies' Literary Society.......	1878	25	
Richmond.	The Cycle..			12
	History Class	1889	50	375
	Tichnor Club.................	1889	25	20
	Tuesday Aftermath...........	1884	1 00	40

Location.	Name.	Date.	Fee.	Mem.
Rochester........	The Woman's League..........	1891	60	35
Rockport.........	Friday Night Club............	1886	N.	
'	The Winteria................	1891	N.	
Rockville	Ladies' Friday Afternoon Club.	1892	...	
Salem...........	Woman's Club.	1891	Ass't	
Shelbyville.......	The Coterie......	1891	N.	
	French History Class.........	1891	60	
	Current Event Club...........	....	....	
	Tourists' Club................	....	....	
	Woman's Club...............	1888	N.	
South Bend.......	Woman's Literary Club.......	1774	Small	30
	Wednesday Club..............	....	....	
Terre Haute......	Saturday Circle...............	....	....	22
	Decorative Art Society.......	....		
	Tuesday Club................	....	....	16
	Young Woman's Club.........	...	....	16
	Woman's Club................	....	....	23
Tipton	LiteraryandEqualSuffrageClub	....	....	
Union City.......	Tichnor Club................	1890	3 00	
Vincennes	The Fortnightly..............	1891	1 00	40
Vevay...........	Eggleston Club	1891	N.	
	Woman's Study Club..........	1888	....	
Wabash.........	Literary and Social Circle.....	1891	Ass't	32
	Round Table..........	1884	50	24
	Symposium...................	1892	50	27

Location.	Name.	Date.	Fee.	Mem.
Warsaw.........	Clio Club	1888	75	35
	Zerelda Reading Club........	1886	....	48
	Warsaw Reading Club........	1880	50	35
Winchester.......	Woman's Wednesday Club.....	1892	25	
	Woman's Club................	1891	....	50
Waterloo.........	Ladies' Minerva Club	....	....	
	X. Y. Z. Club.................	....	....	

WOMEN'S COLLEGE SOCIETIES.

Location.	Name.	Date.	Fee.	Mem.
Greencastle	Theta Alumnæ			
Irvington, Butler Univ.....	Demia Butler	...	...	
	Athenian	....	....	
La Fayette, Purdue Univ...	Philalathean	...	75	40
Moore's Hill......	Sigournian Society	....	....	
Richmond, Earlham College	Phœnix	1856	1 50	
Hanover, Hanover College	Zetelathean	1882	2 00	52
	Christomathean..............	1888	1 50	9

C. L. S. C.—WOMEN.

Location.	Name.	Date.	Fee.	Mem.
Elkhart..........................		1878	50	
Bedford..........................		1892	..	16

MEN'S CLUBS.

Location.	Name.	Date.	Fee.	Mem.
Bloomington	Fortnightly	1891	....	
Crawfordsville ...	Ouiatenon	1883	....	29
	Yandes Coterie	1891	Ass't	15

Location.	Name.	Date.	Fee.	Mem.
Greencastle	Gentlemen's Club	1891	N.	
Hanover	*Union Literary Society	1832	3 00	24
	*Philalathean	1830	2 25	32
Indianapolis	Indianapolis Literary Club ...	1877	10 00	75
	Century Club	1888	9 00	65
Irvington.........	*Philokurian	....	....	
La Fayette	*Emersonian	1887	2 50	26
	*Irving	1875	2 50	33
	*Carlyle	1881	2 50	24
Moore's Hill	*Photozelæn	1869	....	
	*Philoniken.................	....	....	..
Peru	Peru Literary Club...........	1887	2 00	28
	Young Men's Literary Society.	1889	1 00	14
Richmond	The Shakespeare.............	1893	....	
	*Ionian	1857	1 50	
	*Anglican	1890	N.	
Terre Haute......	Gentlemen's Club.............	....	....	

*College Societies.

MIXED CLUBS.

Altoga..........	Mentor Literary and Debating Club	1885	2 00	64
Bedford.	Teachers' Shakespeare Club....	1892	N.	
Bloomingdale.....	*Hesperion..	1862	25	
Bremen	Literary League.............	1892	25	
Brookville	Saturday Club....	1889	....	20
Butlerville.	Audubon Club.	1882		
Dana...........	Excelsior Society....	1891	....	
Decatur.	Shakespeare Club............	....		
Evansville	Clique....................	....		
Frankfort.	Monday Night Club..........	1892	N.	

Location.	Name.	Date.	Fee.	Mem.
Frankfort.	Teachers' Club.	. . . .	N.	
Franklin.	Faculty Club.	1889	N.	
	*Webster	1851	3 00	35
	*Periclesian.	1852	3 00	30
	*Athenian	1884	3 00	31
Greencastle	De Pauw Literary Club.	1890	50	30
	De Pauw University Philological Association	1890	25	
Hobart	Unity Club	. . . .		
Huntingburg. . . .	Huntingburg Literary Society.	1891	15	
Indianapolis	College Corner Club.	1872	. . . .	
	Contemporary Club.	. . . .	. . . .	
	Parlor Club.	1891	1 00	24
	Portfolio Club.	. . .	5 00	40
	Shakespeare Club.	. .	. . . .	
	Hood Literary Society (colored)	1887	. . . .	75
Irvington	Irvington Literary Club.	1890	. . . .	
	The Faculty Club.	. . . .	. . . .	. .
La Fayette.	Parlor Club.	1877	Ass't	32
	Society Ethical Culture	1887	Ass't	12
Lima.	Lima High School Liter'y Soci'y	1891	N.	
Logansport.	Tuesday Night Club.	1890	. . . .	26
	Monday Night Club	. . . .	N.	20
Michigan City	Teachers' Reading Club	. . . .	. . . .	25
Monticello	Monticello Shakespeare Club. .	1892	25	
Mount Vernon . . .	Mount Vernon Literary Society	1890	N.	

Location.	Name.	Date.	Fee.	Mem.
New Castle	Utopian	1892	N.	
Noblesville	Shakespeare Club	1890	1 00	
North Vernon	Emerson Circle	1891	....	14
Oxford	Stanley Club	1892	....	
Odon	Odon Club	1890	50	
Peru	Peru Reading Club	...	....	28
Richmond	The Tourists	1890	1 00	33
	Tuesday Club	1885	1 00	112
Rockville	The Hoosiers	1887	....	27
South Bend	Worth Literary Club	1891		25
Spiceland	Spiceland Literary Club	1880	10	25
Tipton	Friday Evening Club	1892		50
	Literary and Equal Suffrage Club	1887	....	
Union City	Shakespeare Club	1891	25	
Vincennes	Columbia	1889	1 25	

*College Societies.

C. L. S. C.—MIXED.

	Date.	Fee.	Mem.
Tipton	1888	..	50
Alexandria	1892	.50	
Corydon	1891	.50	
Garrett	1892	.50	
Michigan City			15
Remington		...	12
Indianapolis—"Columbian" C. L. S.C	....	.50	
Peru—"Vincent" C. L. S. C	1886	.50	11

TABLE OF STATISTICS.

Women's Clubs	101	
Women's College Societies		8
Men's Clubs	10	
Men's College Societies	...	10
Mixed Clubs	46	
Mixed College Societies	...	4
Number of Clubs	157	
Number of College Societies		22
Whole number of organizations		179

WOMEN'S CLUBS.

Number exclusive of College Societies.		101
Having membership known	....	58
Membership of 58 clubs	1961	
Average membership	....	34
Estimated membership of all	3434	

MEN'S CLUBS.

Number exclusive of College Societies.		10
Having membership known	....	6
Membership of 6 clubs	226	
Average membership	....	37
Estimated membership of all	370	

MIXED CLUBS.

Number exclusive of College Societies.		46
Having membership known	...	18
Membership of 18 clubs	657	
Average membership	36	
Estimated membership of all	1584	
Total estimated membership	5388